Copyright © 1992
by Byron Preiss Visual Publications, Inc.

"Both Sides Now" by Joni Mitchell,
copyright © 1967, 1974 Siquomb Publishing Corp.

This book is based on the lyrics to the song "Both Sides Now" by Joni Mitchell.

Illustrations copyright © 1992
by Alan Baker and Byron Preiss Visual Publications, Inc.
All rights reserved. Published by Scholastic Inc.

SCHOLASTIC HARDCOVER is a registered trademark of Scholastic Inc.

Special thanks to Jean Feiwel, Barbara Marcus, Robin Smith, Judie Castano, and Gloria Boyce.

Editor: Sarah Feldman

Assistant Editor: Kathy Huck

Book Design: Dean Motter

Cover lettering: Anthony Bloch

No part of this publication may be reproduced in whole or in part, or stored
in a retrieval system, or transmitted in any form or by any means, electronic,
mechanical, photocopying , recording, or otherwise,
without written permission of the publisher.
For information regarding permission, write to Scholastic Inc.,
730 Broadway, New York, NY 10003.

Library of Congress Cataloging-in-Publication Data

Mitchell, Joni,
Both sides now / by Joni Mitchell; illustrated by Alan Baker.
p. cm.
Summary : An illustrated version of the Joni Mitchell song, in which clouds,
love, and life itself appear differently when viewed from different perspectives.
ISBN 0- 590-45668-7
1. Children's songs—Texts. [1. Songs.] I. Baker, Alan, ill.
II. Title.
PZ8.3. M677Bo 1992
782. 42164' 0268—dc20   91-36817

CIP

AC

12 11 10 9 8 7 6 5 4 3 2 1   2 3 4 5 6 7/9

Printed in the U.S.A.   36

First Scholastic printing, October 1992

The art in this book was done in watercolor, airbrush, pencil crayon, and bleach.

Joni Mitchell Both Sides Now

Illustrated by Alan Baker

A BYRON PREISS BOOK

SCHOLASTIC
HARDCOVER

SCHOLASTIC INC.
New York

Rows and floes of angel hair

And ice cream castles in the air

And feather canyons everywhere

I've looked at clouds that way;

But now they only block the sun . . . .

They rain and snow on everyone . . .

So many things I would have done

But clouds got in my way.

I've looked at clouds from both sides now,

From up and down, and still somehow . . .

It's clouds' illusions I recall . . .
I really don't know clouds at all.

Moons and Junes and Ferris wheels . . .

The dizzy dancing way you feel

As every fairy tale comes real . . .

I've looked at love that way;

But now it's just another show . . .
You leave them laughing when you go
And if you care, don't let them know . . .
Don't give yourself away!

I've looked at love
from both sides now,
From give and take,
and still somehow . . .
It's love's illusions I recall . . .
I really don't know love at all.

Tears and fears and feeling proud

To say "I love you" right out loud . . .

Dreams and schemes
and circus crowds . . .
I've looked at life that way . . .

But now old friends are acting strange . . .
They shake their heads,
they say I've changed . . .

Well something's lost, but something's gained,

In living every day.

I've looked at life from both sides now,
From win and lose, and still somehow . . .
It's life's illusions I recall . . .
I really don't know life at all!

I've looked at life from both sides now,

From up and down, and still somehow . . .

It's life's illusions I recall . . .

I really don't know life at all!